World Languages

Families in
Polish

Daniel Nunn

Raintree is an imprint of Capstone Global Library Limited, a company incorporated in England and Wales having its registered office at 7 Pilgrim Street, London, EC4V 6LB – Registered company number: 6695582

To contact Raintree please phone 0845 6044371, fax + 44 (0) 1865 312263, or email: myorders@raintreepublishers.co.uk. Customers from outside the UK please telephone +44 1865 312262.

Edited by Daniel Nunn, Rebecca Rissman & Sian Smith
Designed by Joanna Hinton-Malivoire
Picture research by Tracy Cummins
Production by Victoria Fitzgerald
Originated by Capstone Global Library Ltd
Printed and bound in China by Leo Paper Products Ltd

ISBN 978 1 406 25088 6
16 15 14 13 12
10 9 8 7 6 5 4 3 2 1

British Library Cataloguing in Publication Data
Nunn, Daniel.
Families in Polish: rodziny. – (World languages. Families)
1. Polish language–Vocabulary–Pictorial works–Juvenile literature. 2. Families–Poland–Terminology–Pictorial works–Juvenile literature.
I. Title II. Series
491.8'581-dc23

Acknowledgements
We would like to thank the following for permission to reproduce photographs: Shutterstock pp.4 (Catalin Petolea), 5 (optimarc), 5, 6 (Petrenko Andriy), 5, 7 (Tyler Olson), 5, 8 (Andrey Shadrin), 9 (Erika Cross), 10 (Alena Brozova), 5, 11 (Maxim Petrichuk), 12 (auremar), 13 (Mika Heittola), 5, 14, 15 (Alexander Raths), 5, 16 (Samuel Borges), 17 (Vitalii Nesterchuk), 18 (pat138241), 19 (Fotokostic), 20 (Cheryl Casey), 21 (spotmatik).

Cover photographs of two women and a man reproduced with permission of Shutterstock (Yuri Arcurs). Cover photograph of a girl reproduced with permission of istockphoto (© Sean Lockes). Back cover photograph of a girl reproduced with permission of Shutterstock (Erika Cross).

We would like to thank Dorota Holowiak for her invaluable help in the preparation of this book.

Every effort has been made to contact copyright holders of material reproduced in this book. Any omissions will be rectified in subsequent printings if notice is given to the publisher.

Contents

Cześć!

Mam na imię Daniel.

My name is Daniel.

A to jest moja rodzina.

And this is my family.

Moja matka i mój ojciec

moja matka

To jest moja matka.

This is my mother.

To jest mój ojciec.

This is my father.

Mój brat i moja siostra

mój brat

To jest mój brat.

This is my brother.

To jest moja siostra.

This is my sister.

Moja macocha i mój ojczym

moja macocha

To jest moja macocha.

This is my step-mother.

mój ojczym

To jest mój ojczym.

This is my step-father.

Mój brat przyrodni i moja siostra przyrodnia

mój brat przyrodni

To jest mój brat przyrodni.

This is my step-brother.

moja siostra przyrodnia

To jest moja siostra przyrodnia.

This is my step-sister.

Moja babcia i mój dziadek

moja babcia

To jest moja babcia.

This is my grandmother.

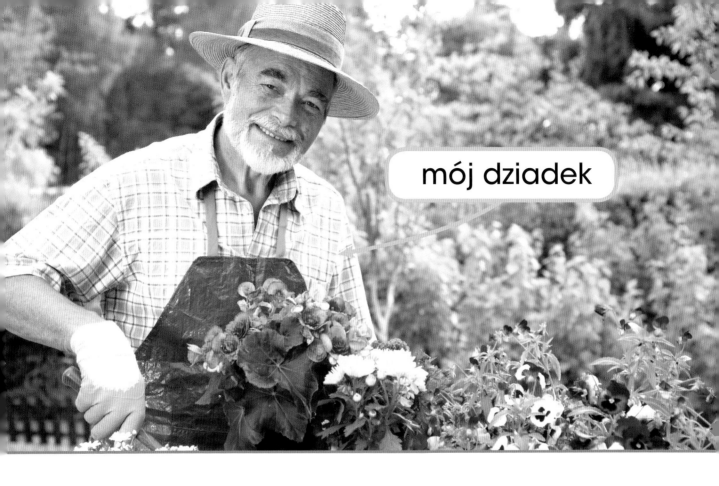

mój dziadek

To jest mój dziadek.

This is my grandfather.

Moja ciotka i mój wujek

moja ciotka

To jest moja ciotka.

This is my aunt.

mój wujek

To jest mój wujek.

This is my uncle.

Moi kuzyni

moja kuzynka

To są moi kuzyni.

These are my cousins.

mój kuzyn

19

Moi przyjaciele

moja przyjaciółka

To są moi przyjaciele.

These are my friends.

mój przyjaciel

21

Dictionary

Polish word	How to say it	English word
a	ah	and
babcia	bahb-tsah	grandmother
brat	braht	brother
brat przyrodni	braht ph-shee-rohd-nih	step-brother
ciotka	tsioh-tkah	aunt
cześć	tcheh-sih-tsih	hi
dziadek	djiah-deck	grandfather
i	eh	and
kuzyn	coo-zihn	cousin (male)
kuzyni	coo-zih-nih	cousins
kuzynka	coo-zihn-kah	cousin (female)
macocha	mah-tsoh-chah	step-mother
mam na imię	mahm nah ee-meeh	my name is
matka	maht-kah	mother
moi	moh-eh	my (plural)
mój	moo-y	my (male)

Polish word	How to say it	English word
moja	moh-yah	my (female)
ojciec	oh-ey-tseh-ts	father
ojczym	oh-ey-chih-m	step-father
przyjaciel	ph-shee-yah-tsehl	friend (male)
przyjaciele	ph-shee-yah-tseh-leh	friends
przyjaciółka	ph-shee-yah-tsoow-kah	friend (female)
rodzina	roh-djeh-nah	family
siostra	sioh-strah	sister
siostra przyrodnia	sioh-strah	
	ph-shee-rohd-niah	step-sister
to jest	toh yehst	this is
to są	toh sohm	these are
wujek	voo-yehk	uncle

See words in the "How to say it" columns for a rough guide to pronunciations.

Index

Notes for parents and teachers

In Polish, nouns are either masculine, feminine, or neuter. There are no words for 'the' or 'a' in Polish. Sometimes pronouns ('my') have different spellings, depending on whether the noun is masculine or feminine or whether the noun is in singular or plural form, which is why some of the words have more than one spelling.